THE DIFFERENCE BETWEEN MEN AND WOMEN

By

FRED SAHNER

Illustrated By

LENNIE PETERSON

Published by

CCC Publications
9725 Lurline Avenue
Chatsworth, CA 91311

Manufactured in the United States of America

Cover ©1999 CCC Publications

Interior illustrations ©1999 CCC Publications

Cover/Interior art by Lennie Peterson

Cover/Interior production by Klaus Selbrede

ISBN: 1-57644-081-8

If your local U.S. bookstore is out of stock, copies of this book may be obtained by mailing check or money order for $6.95 per book (plus $3.00 to cover postage and handling) to:
CCC Publications; 9725 Lurline Avenue, Chatsworth, CA 91311

Pre-publication Edition – 1/99
First Printing - 7/99

DEDICATION
To Barbara and Ed, Lisa and Ken, and Pat and Ed

INTRODUCTION

Life's Rule #1...
The Opposite Sex can *NEVER be understood!*
(until now)

Finally, a book that explains THAT OTHER SEX. The one with all the bizarre habits, strange ideas and disconnected brain cells. In these pages, you'll find the answer to what THAT OTHER GENDER wants in almost every situation.

Men and Women differ in every possible way, including: values, attitudes, opinions, outlooks, and beliefs. Probably the only thing we do agree on is both of us hate alarm clocks. While we are always intelligent, loving, kind, sincere and thoughtful, THAT OTHER SEX is out there disproving Evolution. If anything, THEY seem to be going backwards. Let's face it; as a group, THEY'RE barely housebroken. Can you believe it; we're supposed to mate with THOSE PEOPLE. Is life unfair or what?

However, the pages ahead will help you to almost understand THEM, but total understanding is totally out of the question. So, let's appreciate THAT OTHER SEX for what joy they bring us; they are trying you know. And what a scary thought that is.

PHILOSOPHY OF LIFE

For Women — Life is like a rainbow . . . beautiful, inspiring and waiting to be enjoyed.

For Men — Life is like an inner tube . . . slippery, fragile and just waiting to blow up in your face.

DREAM TRIPS

Those exotic ports we long to visit have one thing in common: they cause big arguments. A man and a woman simply can't agree on *what* constitutes a dream trip.

Dream trips . . .

For Women	*For Men*
London	Auto Showroom
Rome	Local Bar
Hawaii	The Garage
Paris	Hardware Store

Fantasy

For Women —

Alone in a room with ten TV Soap Opera hunks – each one vying for her love.

For Men —

Alone in a room with ten TVs – each one tuned to a different game.

Shopping

In any large department store you will always find the merchandise, strategically placed.

Retailers know what their customers want and how they shop. That's why department stores have the following layout.

Women's Section
Floors 1, 2, 3, 4, 5
The Basement
The Sub-basement
Tables outside the store
The Air Ducts
The Loading Dock

Men's Section
A small table (3 inches from the front door)

SECRET TALENTS

WOMEN: Can prepare a five course meal for ten people in one hour.

MEN: Can set the Microwave for 'Popcorn' with his eyes closed.

HAPPINESS

7 THINGS THAT MAKE A WOMAN HAPPY

Being less than 10 pounds overweight

Hearing, "I love you"

Fitting into last year's bathing suit

Eating out

Surprise presents

Getting high marks on a 'Cosmo' test

7 THINGS THAT MAKE A MAN HAPPY

Not having to shave

Not needing a bigger pants

Flattery

Afternoon naps

Shopping

The '3 Ps' . . . Pretzels, pizza and prime ribs

Fixing something and it doesn't immediately fall apart again

Having fifty dollars 'Mad Money' tucked in his wallet

HOUSE CLEANING

Nowhere do the sexes diverge more sharply, than in the area of cleaning the home.

To **Women** *House Cleaning means:*

dusting, mopping, scrubbing, vacuuming, washing, wiping, straightening, rubbing, rinsing, and picking up.

To **Men** *House Cleaning means:*

not making the house any dirtier than it is.

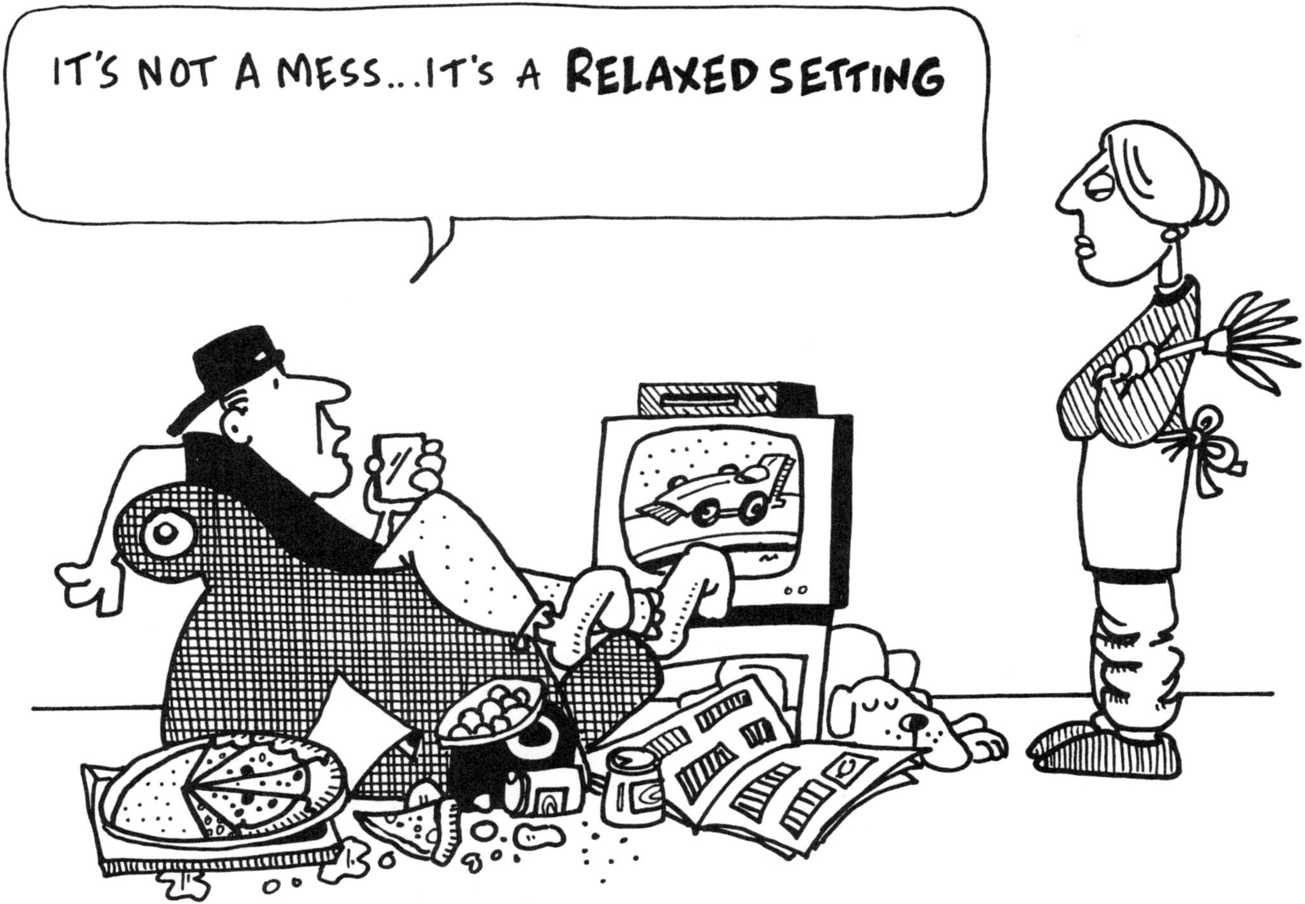
IT'S NOT A MESS...IT'S A RELAXED SETTING

FRIENDS

Men and Women seek special qualities when choosing friends.

Life long associations are built on having these characteristics.

QUALITIES THEY WANT IN FRIENDS

WOMEN

Open
Reliable
Thoughtful
Kind
Supportive
Understanding
Good Humored
And a little less attractive than themselves

MEN

A person who won't ask you
a lot of personal stuff

A person who won't tell you a lot
of personal stuff

ROMANCE

FOR A **WOMAN**, ROMANCE BEGINS . . .

When he brings her flowers

FOR A **MAN**, ROMANCE BEGINS . . .

When he un-hooks her bra

TRACKING THE IMPORTANT DATES

The sexes share responsibilities in keeping track of life's milestones.

Women keep track of: All birthdays, all anniversaries, all special occasions, all holidays.

Men keep track of: Opening day for Football, baseball, basketball, fishing and hunting season.

BATHROOM HABITS

A man and woman can happily live together *if* they have separate bathrooms. Marriage counselors claim, shared bathrooms are the leading cause of divorce in America.

WOMEN VIEW BATHROOMS: as extended dressing rooms, a place to store several thousand tiny bottles, four hair dryers (only one of which works), and a bathtub for brief (4 hour) periods of lounging.

MEN VIEW BATHROOMS: as a good place to read, search for gray hair, or search for any hair, take ten-second showers. And a chance to check the mirror for possible muscle sightings.

THE SUPERMARKET SHOPPING LIST

THE MALE LIST   VS.   **THE FEMALE LIST**

THE MALE LIST	THE FEMALE LIST
Dozen Beef Jerkies	Low-Salt Turkey breast
Ring Dings	Organically grown Apples
Aspirin	Vitamins
8 Six-packs of beer	8 bottles of mountain spring water
Axle grease remover	Dove soap
Dozen bagels with a smear	Whole-wheat seven-grain bread
Gal. of Chocolate Fudge Ice Cream	Cup of fat free Jello
Extra heavy cream	.01% Skim milk
Instant coffee	Colombian special premium blend
(All in a plastic bag)	(All in a recycled paper bag)

WORK

Women see work as . . .
- A place to earn spending money
- A place to make free phone calls
- A place to hear gossip
- A place to meet guys
- A place to kick a hole in the 'Glass Ceiling'

Men see work as . . .
- A place to start an 'Office Pool'
- A place to cool off on hot days
- A place to get free pens
- A place to meet women
- Something to do until the weekend

WHEN SICK

Women keep going.

Men keep going, until they reach the bedroom where they can: lie down, groan, moan, nap, snap and expect to be waited on.

THEIR HEROES

The traditional heroes of the sexes are . . .

FOR WOMEN	FOR MEN
Susan B. Anthony	John Wayne
Florence Nightingale	Michael Jordan
Elizabeth Cady Stanton	Spider-Man
Harriet Beecher Stowe	Indiana Jones
Sandra Day O'Connor	Willie Nelson
Madame Curie	Clint Eastwood

DIETING

How WOMEN handle weight problems . . .
- They get their hair cut real short
- They wear dresses five sizes too large, so they appear to be losing weight
- If they don't actually get to Weight Watchers, they at least find out where it is
- They set a firm starting date to begin their diet. Typical dates are: next week, the first of the month, in the Spring, and when pigs fly

How MEN handle weight problems . . .
- They go on the miracle 'All Beer Diet'
- They stop eating caviar, and cut way back on Escargo
- They watch TV exercise shows that feature buxom women in skimpy leotards
- They exercise for three minutes, then declare themselves fit for another year

Money

Women: Spend money wisely; they seek out sales and shop, and shop and shop and . . .

Men: *Would* spend money wisely, except they can't be bothered with looking for sales or bargains. (How do you think the price of a new car got to $30,000 anyway?)

LIFETIME GOALS

For Women: To learn, to grow, to be the best person she can be. To leave the world a better place than she found it. And, to always take a smaller dress size than her girlfriends.

For Men: To find a woman with high tolerance and low expectations.

TIME

As a rule: *men run late and women run later.*

Women can't understand why men get upset when they're late. After all, even if you only make the plane by hanging from a wing . . . at least you'll be the *first* person off.

EATING OUT

Both sexes enjoy eating out, but for very different reasons.

What WOMEN enjoy about eating out:

Not having to cook

Getting dressed up

Being waited on

Trying new foods

Attractive surroundings

A chance to sit through an entire meal

No dishes to wash

Stealing packs of Sweet 'N Low

What MEN enjoy about eating out:

Checking out the waitresses

CELEBRATING BIRTHDAYS

Both sexes enjoy the attention that birthdays bring.
But, they do make one request of their wellwishers.

For Women . . .

Please don't mention *how old they are*

For Men . . .

Please don't mention *how old they look*

S──EX

Along with ice cream and potato chips, sex is one of life's essentials, a true prime mover. There are two kinds of sex: **Wonderful** and **Fantastic**. Anyone who says they don't enjoy making love, must be confusing it with another activity. Such as push-ups.

WHAT WOMEN ENJOY ABOUT SEX: The tenderness, the words of love, the gentle foreplay, the touching, a chance to hug and caress. A long build up to a thundering climax. Laying spent in her lover's arms.

WHAT MEN ENJOY ABOUT SEX:
Everything except the mushy stuff.

TAKING A TRIP

Long car trips call for careful planning and good directions. Of course that *other* sex will have their own, misguided idea, of what constitutes good directions.

Typical directions a *WOMAN* insists on having:
1) Back out of driveway
2) Look both ways . . . proceed
3) Go East on Route 90 (that's toward Europe)
4) Go 6.01781 miles to Exit 11
   (situated between exits 10 and 12)
5) Exit at exit 11 exit
6) Make a right at the corner (where you'll see 'Adrian's Hair and Nail Salon, Inc.')
7) Go 3 and 1/8 blocks
8) Stop car. You are there.

Typical *MAN* directions:
1) Head East
2) Wing it.

THE PERFECT MEAL

Food is such an important part of life, that many of us can't live without it. How we yearn for that perfect meal. The right combination of food and drink, followed by more food and more drink.

Of course men and women have different takes on this tasty subject.

A *Woman's* perfect meal includes:

> Salad, water and clean utensils

A *Man's* perfect meal includes:

> A basket of bread, two bars of butter, fried anything, the entire desert cart and a bartender with a heavy hand

WHAT THEY HAVE TO HAVE

What *WOMEN* think they *must* have

- Unlimited use of the bathroom
- 284 recipes for pasta
- Reliable telephone
- Comfortable shoes
- A friendly scale
- A user-friendly man

What *MEN* think they *must* have

- A *BIG* screen TV
- A comfortable chair
- Reliable screwdriver
- 74 Tee-shirts
- A large coffee mug
- A user-friendly woman

DECORATING

Men and women have totally different interests when it comes to decorating the home.

Women are concerned with: Style, color, space, fabric, lighting, mood, and design.

Men are concerned with: Shortening the distance between the couch and the refrigerator.

DRESSING UP

Great care goes into our attire. Both sexes know clothes say a lot about the wearer. This is especially true when dressing for a special occasion.

For *WOMEN* the attire considerations are:
— Dress (Must be new and cost twice what she can afford)
— Shoes (Must be new, uncomfortable and a famous brand name)
— Jewelry (Tasteful, expensive and envy provoking)
— Pocketbook (Large enough to carry two hundred vital make-up accessories)

For *MEN* the attire considerations are:
— Pants (Roomy in case he eats a big meal)
— Shirt (Clean, white and with no more than three missing buttons)
— Shoes (Comfortable, with at least 3,000 miles on them)
— Socks (The good pair, the ones with the small holes)

RETIREMENT GOALS

For Women: A chance to pursue a hobby, such as: painting, hiking and gardening.

For Men: A chance to pursue a hobby, such as: resting, napping and complaining.

DECISION MAKING

HOW *WOMEN* MAKE DECISIONS

Women see a problem and quickly make a decision. However, before announcing their decision, they bounce it off a few trusted intimates, such as: her eighty-five closest friends, any cousins with a telephone, her favorite bank teller, a stranger on line at the supermarket, her hairdresser and anyone else who'll stop to listen.

Some women simplify this process, by asking themselves what a man would do, and then do the opposite.

HOW *MEN* MAKE DECISIONS

Men consider a problem from every angle, they weigh the possibilities and mull over every conceivable option.

Only when he is satisfied that he's explored every possible solution does he reach into his pocket, pull out a coin and call *heads* or *tails*.

HEALTH

To take care of their health, *Women*:

Have regular check-ups, eat healthy foods, take vitamins and exercise by continuously shopping.

To take care of their health, *Men*:

Weasel out of their yearly check-ups, gobble junk food and stay physically fit by working the TV remote control.

EAT SLOW, MARTY... THE EXPIRATION DATE IS JULY, 2045
double YUMS Whoopee Sugar Treats

RAISING CHILDREN

Each parent brings special skills to the task of raising children.

WHAT *WOMEN* TEACH CHILDREN

- Which foods to eat
- The importance of good hygiene
- That hard work brings success
- To wear clean underwear
  (In the event of an accident,
  you won't embarrass the family)

WHAT *MEN* TEACH CHILDREN

- Where to get a good deal on tires
- How to sleep any time, any place
- Which baseball team to root for
- How to hear only what you
  want to hear

SON, IT'S TIME TO TEACH YOU AN IMPORTANT MALE SECRET...
HOW TO **LOOK** BUSY WHILE DOING ABSOLUTELY NOTHING

FAVORITE MUSIC

For *women*: Love songs celebrating eternal devotion.

For *men*: Country and Western songs about driving an 18 wheeler cross-country with either a big dog or a bad woman at your side.

CELEBRATING ANNIVERSARIES

A man will always remember an anniversary . . . as long as you remind him the day before.

HOW *WOMEN* LIKE TO CELEBRATE AN ANNIVERSARY

- Buying a new dress
- Dining at a fancy restaurant
- Drinking Champagne
- Receiving an expensive gift
- Being told they are loved

HOW *MEN* LIKE TO CELEBRATE AN ANNIVERSARY

- Remembering those happy days, before there were any anniversaries

THE AGE WE REACH MATURITY

FOR *WOMEN*:   18.

At which time they realize that Prince Charming is a fictional character, and that Freddy Krueger is all too real.

FOR *MEN*:   68.

At which time they realize they will never play quarterback for the Dallas Cowboys or make love to a Dallas Cowgirl.

STAYING IN SHAPE

Each sex is firmly committed (sort of) to reducing flab.

A *WOMAN'S* FAVORITE WORKOUT INCLUDES:
* Searching for miracle diets
* Reading diet books by movie stars, who explain how they lost that pesky 3 ounces
* Buying magazines with cover stories proclaiming, 'How to lose 149 pounds in 7 days, on **The Miracle *All Chocolate* Diet!**'

A *MAN'S* FAVORITE WORKOUT INCLUDES:
* Carrying cases of beer into the house
* Fidgeting around while standing in line at the Dairy Queen
* Watching 'X' rated movies, that *really* make him sweat

COOKING

WOMEN BELIEVE: that preparing a meal takes the proper ingredients, a fabulous recipe, and careful attention to detail.

MEN BELIEVE: that cooking consists of two choices: take out *or* send out

FANTASY SEX

FEMALE SEX FANTASIES INCLUDE:

- A handsome stranger
- A luxurious setting
- A heart-shaped bed
- Two hours of foreplay
- Soft music
- Moonlight
- Satin sheets
- Champagne
- Lingering kisses
- Gentle fingers
- Words of love
- Five orgasms

MALE SEX FANTASIES INCLUDE:

- A willing partner

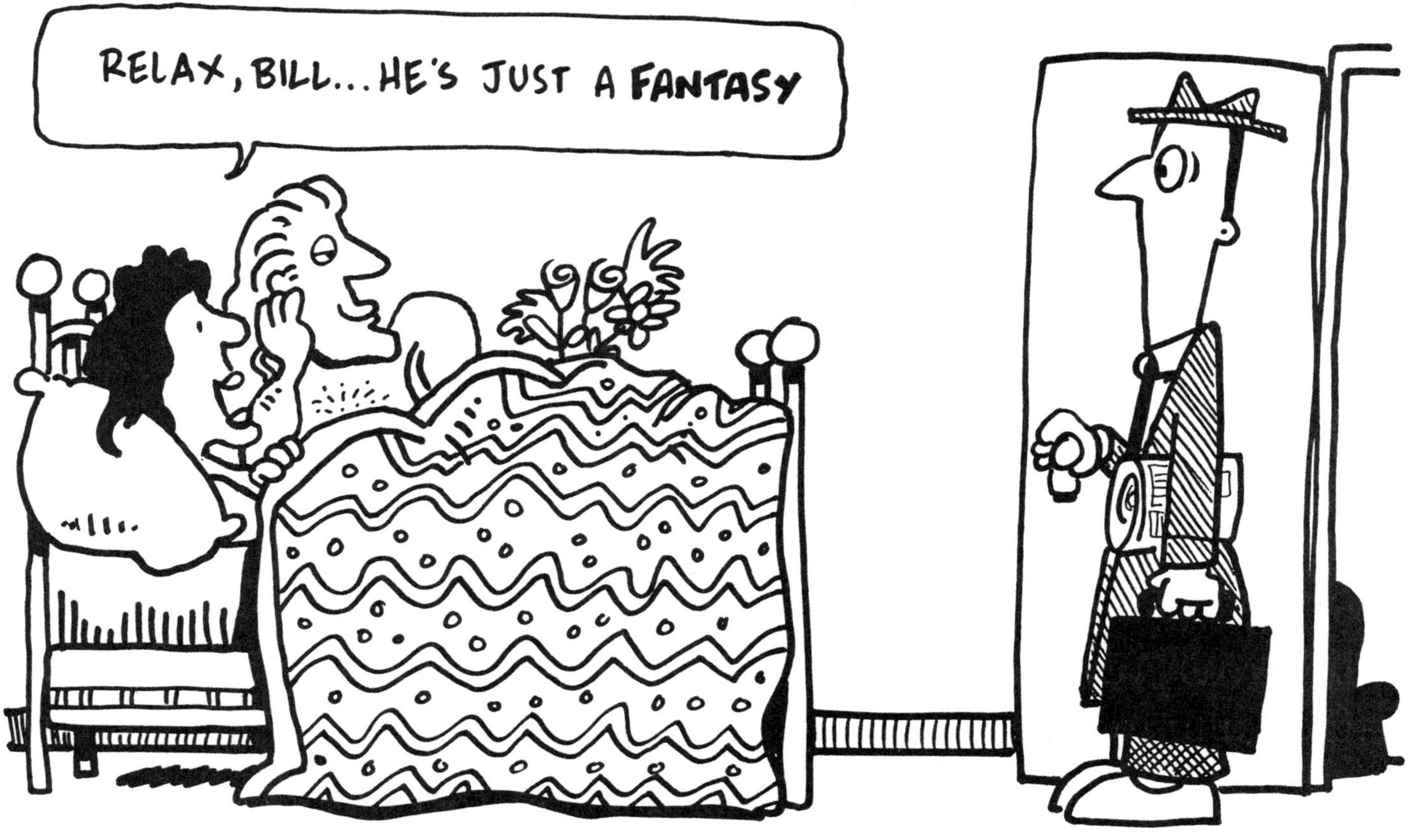
RELAX, BILL... HE'S JUST A FANTASY

In a Crisis

WOMEN IN A CRISIS....

Do what's needed.

And if they don't know what to do, they get help.

MEN IN A CRISIS.....

Often don't know what to do, but they charge ahead and act anyway. In a real *crisis*, such as noticing hair loss or running out of chips and beer, men are helpless and inconsolable.

COMMUNICATING

Women communicate! They talk to family, friends, strangers, pets and coffee pots (with varying results). Secrets have a short lifetime when women meet. News is "the scoop" and it must be passed along. Friends *must* know what you know. Yes, dirt travels faster than light.

Men strive to be the strong silent type, well the silent type anyway, and they speak mainly to themselves. Men have trouble being 'open'. If you ask a man how he's doing, invariably the answer will be, "Great!" He'll say that, even if he's just lost his job, been abandoned by his wife and has the entire F. B. I. after him.

HOME REPAIR

Women believe that when a repair job exceeds your level of ability, you should hire a qualified repairman, (or to be P. C., a *'repairperson'*).

Men believe you call for help *only* if water is cascading out of every pipe in the house, and Halibut are swimming around the living room.

ENTERTAINMENT

The sexes enjoy their leisure hours in *very* different ways.

WOMEN PREFER

- Movies with inspiring messages
- Plays with high drama
- Listening to romantic music
- Museums
- Concerts
- Public Television
- Piano recitals
- Reading great books

MEN PREFER

- Movies with shoot-outs and car chases
- Plays with full frontal nudity
- Songs about dying cowboys
- Parks with rollercoaster rides
- Chug-a-lug contests
- Demolition Derby night on ESPN
- Listening to someone play 'Chopsticks'
- Booking great bets

At the Beach

The sexes behave *very* differently at the beach.

For instance . . .

Women wear bikinis the size of Band-Aids and then get mad when guys gawk at them. Bathing beauty wannabes never go into water that's over their ankles or associate with anyone crude enough to splash them.

Men hold in their stomachs, attempt to look athletic by tossing around a football and refuse to nap. They don't want to miss any well-packed bikini tops passing by.

PLANNING

A *WOMAN* PLANS . . . by making a comprehensive, thorough, well-considered, very specific list . . . *which she then loses.*

A *MAN* PLANS . . . by *finding* the woman's lost list.

DISAGREEMENTS

Differing opinions are a part of life. So, it's only natural that men and women will see things differently. And that's when it gets interesting.

WHEN *WOMEN* ARGUE WITH MEN THEY . . .
Quote Martha Stewart and hang tough until they get their way

WHEN *MEN* ARGUE WITH WOMEN THEY . . .
Fume, mumble and finally give in (if they hope to have sex *ever again*)

AMBITION

A *WOMAN'S* AMBITION:

- To find love

- To have good friends

- To have a job she enjoys
- To have a nice big home

A *MAN'S* AMBITION:

- To find a woman who understands the 'point spread'

- To have someone call him, 'A Hunk'

- To visit a Harley Davidson plant
- To have a TV so big it barely fits inside his home

COMPLIMENTS

Well, some people can give compliments and others can't. You don't have to guess who'd have trouble in this area . . . do you?

A TYPICAL *WOMAN'S* COMPLIMENT –

"I love that dress on you. It's your color. You look fantastic!"

A TYPICAL *MAN'S* COMPLIMENT –

*"Hey, that's **not** the worst dress I've seen you wear!"*

TRAVEL

Packing for a trip presents a MAJOR gap in behavior between the sexes. For example, here's what we pack for a weekend trip.

WOMEN PACK
- 5 dresses
- 4 blazers
- 11 pair of stockings
- 3 bottles of hand cream
- 4 lipsticks
- 2 robes
- 7 skirts
- 7 panties
- 2 hair dryers
- 4 bottles of body lotion
- 1 cell phone
- 3 bathing suits
- 7 blouses
- 5 bras
- 6 pair of earrings
- 7 pairs of shoes
- 3 nightgowns

MEN PACK
- 1 Tee-shirt
- 1 pair of socks (optional)
- 1 pair of cut-offs
- 1 pack of gum
- 1 baseball cap

Vacations

While everyone loves a vacation . . . there are BIG differences in what we enjoy.

Here are our ideal vacations:

For *Women*	**For *Men***
Harrison Ford's bedroom	A Ford showroom
The Beach at Maui	The Beach at Baywatch
Camping with Mr. Universe	Camping with the guys
New York at Christmas	Las Vegas at Halloween
Fabio's cabin in the woods	A bar stool near the jukebox

BREAKING UP

The end of a relationship can be especially painful. Finding the right words of parting takes thought, compassion and tact.
A typical brush off , sounds like this:

A Woman says . . .

"I'm very sorry, but this just isn't working out. We're in different places and I'd like it to stay that way. Like, Lance and Heather, on 'Guiding Light', we're not meant to be. Please, when you think of me, remember the good times; that's if you can think of any good times. So, goodbye dear friend, . . . Au Voir, ciao!"

A *Man* says . . .

"I'm outta here!"

THE BIGGEST DIFFERENCE

A *Woman* believes . . .

To love someone is *worth* all the trouble

A *Man* believes . . .

To love someone is the *cause* of all trouble

TITLES BY CCC PUBLICATIONS

Blank Books ($3.99)
SEX AFTER BABY
SEX AFTER 30
SEX AFTER 40
SEX AFTER 50

Retail $4.95 – $4.99
"?" book
CAN SEX IMPROVE YOUR GOLF?
THE COMPLETE BOOGER BOOK
FLYING FUNNIES
MARITAL BLISS & OXYMORONS
THE ADULT DOT-TO-DOT BOOK
THE DEFINITIVE FART BOOK
THE COMPLETE WIMP'S GUIDE TO SEX
THE CAT OWNER'S SHAPE UP MANUAL
THE OFFICE FROM HELL
FITNESS FANATICS
YOUNGER MEN ARE BETTER THAN RETIN-A
BUT OSSIFER, IT'S NOT MY FAULT
YOU KNOW YOU'RE AN OLD FART WHEN...
1001 WAYS TO PROCRASTINATE
HORMONES FROM HELL II
SHARING THE ROAD WITH IDIOTS
THE GREATEST ANSWERING MACHINE MESSAGES
WHAT DO WE DO NOW??
HOW TO TALK YOU WAY OUT OF A TRAFFIC TICKET
THE BOTTOM HALF
LIFE'S MOST EMBARRASSING MOMENTS
HOW TO ENTERTAIN PEOPLE YOU HATE
YOUR GUIDE TO CORPORATE SURVIVAL
NO HANG-UPS (Volumes I, II & III – $3.95 ea.)
TOTALLY OUTRAGEOUS BUMPER-SNICKERS ($2.95)

Retail $5.95
30 – DEAL WITH IT!
40 – DEAL WITH IT!
50 – DEAL WITH IT!
60 – DEAL WITH IT!
OVER THE HILL – DEAL WITH IT!
SLICK EXCUSES FOR STUPID SCREW-UPS
SINGLE WOMEN VS. MARRIED WOMEN
TAKE A WOMAN'S WORD FOR IT
SEXY CROSSWORD PUZZLES
SO, YOU'RE GETTING MARRIED
YOU KNOW HE'S A WOMANIZING SLIMEBALL WHEN...
GETTING OLD SUCKS
WHY GOD MAKES BALD GUYS
OH BABY!
PMS CRAZED: TOUCH ME AND I'LL KILL YOU!
WHY MEN ARE CLUELESS
THE BOOK OF WHITE TRASH
THE ART OF MOONING
GOLFAHOLICS
CRINKLED 'N' WRINKLED
SMART COMEBACKS FOR STUPID QUESTIONS
YIKES! IT'S ANOTHER BIRTHDAY
SEX IS A GAME
SEX AND YOUR STARS
SIGNS YOUR SEX LIFE IS DEAD
MALE BASHING: WOMEN'S FAVORITE PASTIME
THINGS YOU CAN DO WITH A USELESS MAN
MORE THINGS YOU CAN DO WITH A USELESS MAN
RETIREMENT: THE GET EVEN YEARS
LITTLE INSTRUCTION BOOK OF THE RICH & FAMOUS
WELCOME TO YOUR MIDLIFE CRISIS
GETTING EVEN WITH THE ANSWERING MACHINE
ARE YOU A SPORTS NUT?
MEN ARE PIGS / WOMEN ARE BITCHES
THE BETTER HALF
ARE WE DYSFUNCTIONAL YET?
TECHNOLOGY BYTES!
50 WAYS TO HUSTLE YOUR FRIENDS

HORMONES FROM HELL
HUSBANDS FROM HELL
KILLER BRAS & Other Hazards Of The 50's
IT'S BETTER TO BE OVER THE HILL THAN UNDER IT
HOW TO REALLY PARTY!!!
WORK SUCKS!
THE PEOPLE WATCHER'S FIELD GUIDE
THE ABSOLUTE LAST CHANCE DIET BOOK
THE UGLY TRUTH ABOUT MEN
NEVER A DULL CARD
THE LITTLE BOOK OF ROMANTIC LIES

Retail $6.95
CYBERGEEK IS CHIC
THE DIFFERENCE BETWEEN MEN AND WOMEN
GO TO HEALTH!
NOT TONIGHT, DEAR, I HAVE A COMPUTER!
THINGS YOU WILL NEVER HEAR THEM SAY
THE SENIOR CITIZENS'S SURVIVAL GUIDE
IT'S A MAD MAD MAD SPORTS WORLD
THE LITTLE BOOK OF CORPORATE LIES
RED HOT MONOGAMY
LOVE DAT CAT
HOW TO SURVIVE A JEWISH MOTHER

Retail $7.95
WHY MEN DON'T HAVE A CLUE
LADIES, START YOUR ENGINES!
ULI STEIN'S "ANIMAL LIFE"
ULI STEIN'S "I'VE GOT IT BUT IT'S JAMMED"
ULI STEIN'S "THAT SHOULD NEVER HAVE HAPPENED"

NO HANG-UPS – CASSETTES Retail $5.98
Vol. I: GENERAL MESSAGES (M or F)
Vol. II: BUSINESS MESSAGES (M or F)
Vol. III: 'R' RATED MESSAGES (M or F)
Vol. V: CELEBRI-TEASE